PIANO • VOCAL • GUITAR

3rd Edition

THE DEFINITIVE

COLLECTION

127 Songs

S0-DYR-489

ISBN 0-7935-1985-3

HAL•LEONARD®
CORPORATION
7777 W. BLUEMOUND RD. P.O. BOX 13819 MILWAUKEE, WI 53213

Visit Hal Leonard Online at
www.halleonard.com

THE DEFINITIVE

Christmas

COLLECTION

A CAROLING WE GO

Music and Lyrics by
JOHNNY MARKS

ANGELS FROM THE REALMS OF GLORY

Words by JAMES MONTGOMERY
Music by HENRY T. SMART

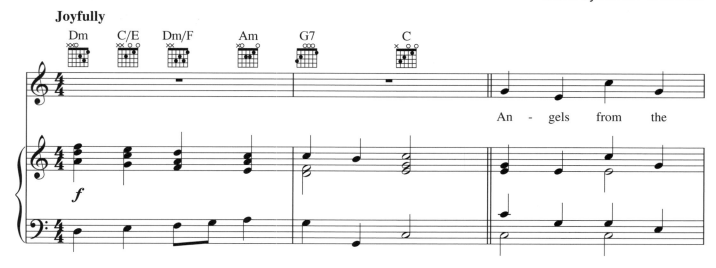

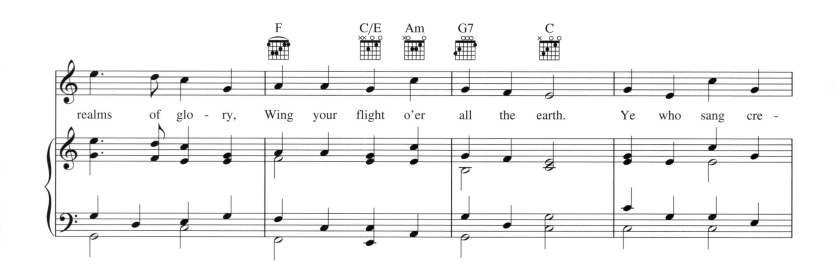

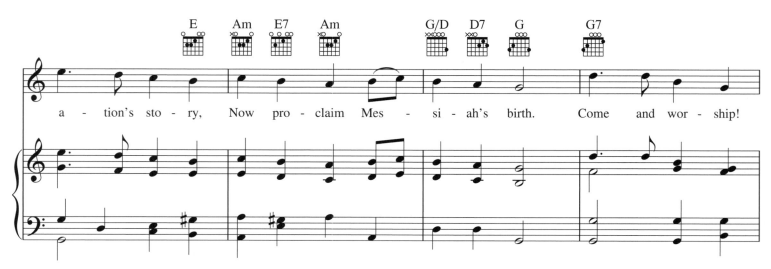

ANGELS WE HAVE HEARD ON HIGH

Traditional French Carol
Translated by JAMES CHADWICK

AS WITH GLADNESS MEN OF OLD

Words by WILLIAM CHATTERTON DIX
Music by CONRAD KOCHER

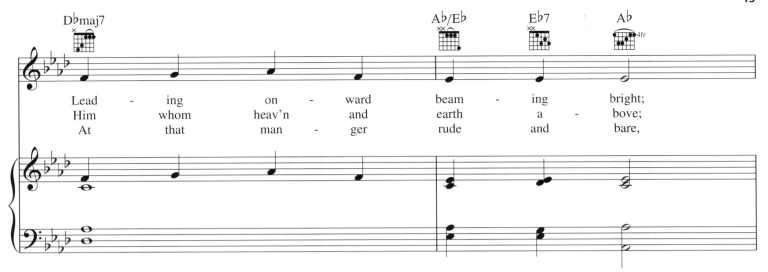

Lead - ing on - ward beam - ing bright;
Him whom heav'n and earth a - bove;
At that man - ger rude and bare,

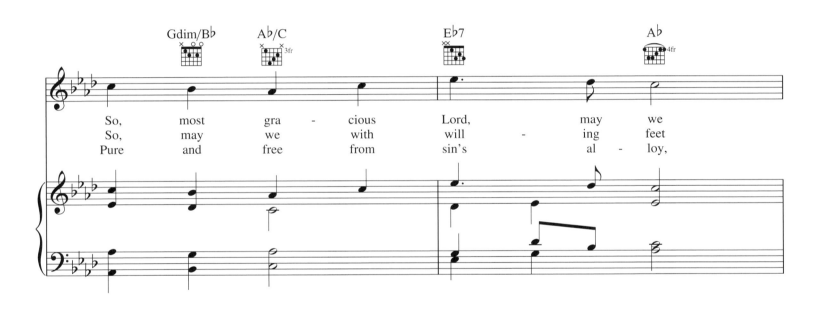

So, most gra - cious Lord, may we
So, may we free with from sin's al - ing feet
Pure and free from sin's al - loy,

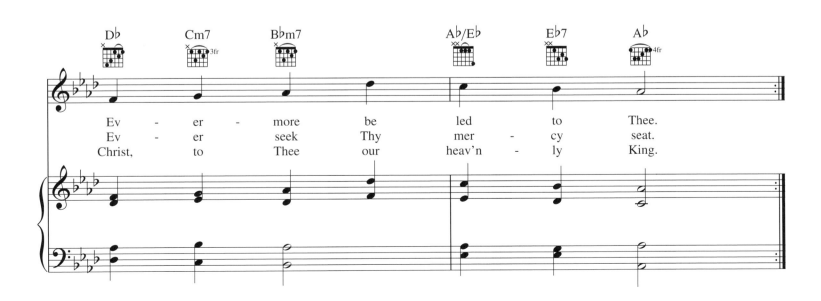

Ev - er - more be led to Thee.
Ev - er seek Thy mer - cy seat.
Christ, to Thee our heav'n - ly King.

ASPENGLOW

Words and Music by
JOHN DENVER

See the sun-light through the pine, taste the warm of win-ter wine,
As the win-ter days un-fold, hearts grow warm-er with the cold,

dream of soft-ly fall-ing snow, }
peace of mind is all you know, } win-ter sköl, As-pen-glow.

As-pen is a life to live, see how much there is to give,

AULD LANG SYNE

Words by ROBERT BURNS
Traditional Scottish Melody

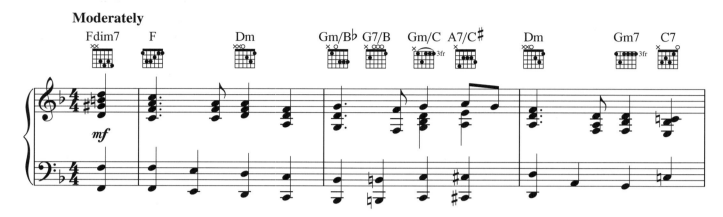

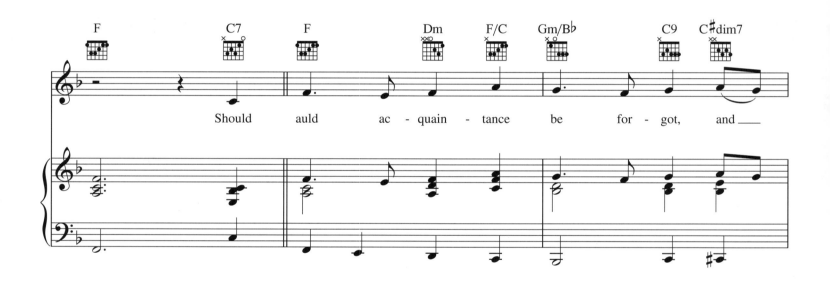

Should auld ac-quain-tance be for-got, and ___

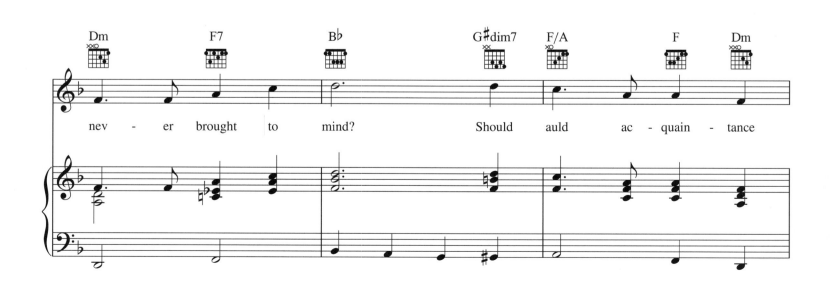

nev - er brought to mind? Should auld ac-quain-tance

AWAY IN A MANGER

Traditional
Words by JOHN T. McFARLAND (v.3)
Music by WILLIAM J. KIRKPATRICK

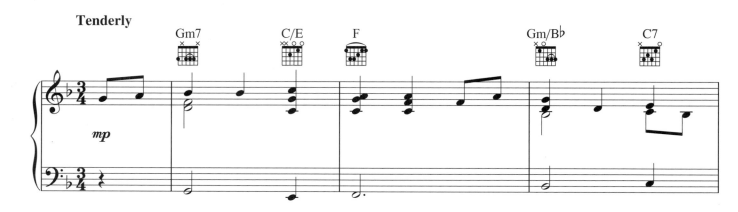

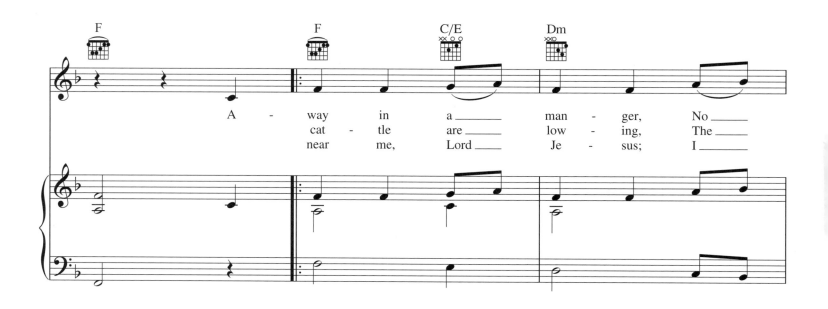

A- way in a _____ man- ger, No _____
cat- tle are _____ low- ing, The _____
near me, Lord _____ Je- sus; I _____

crib for a bed, The _____ lit- tle Lord
ba - by a - wakes, But _____ lit- tle Lord
ask Thee to stay Close _____ by me for-

AWAY IN A MANGER

Traditional
Words by JOHN T. McFARLAND (v.3)
Music by JAMES R. MURRAY

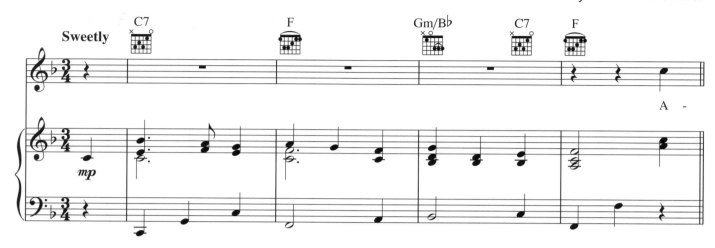

21

Because It's Christmas
(For All the Children)

Music by BARRY MANILOW
Lyric by BRUCE SUSSMAN and JACK FELDMAN

Moderately slow

BLUE CHRISTMAS

Words and Music by BILLY HAYES
and JAY JOHNSON

THE BOAR'S HEAD CAROL

Traditional English

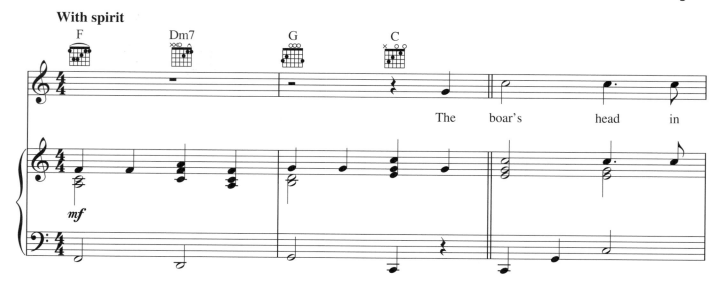

With spirit

The boar's head in

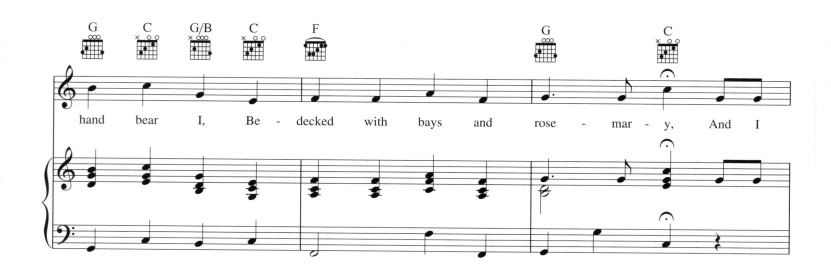

hand bear I, Be - decked with bays and rose - mar - y, And I

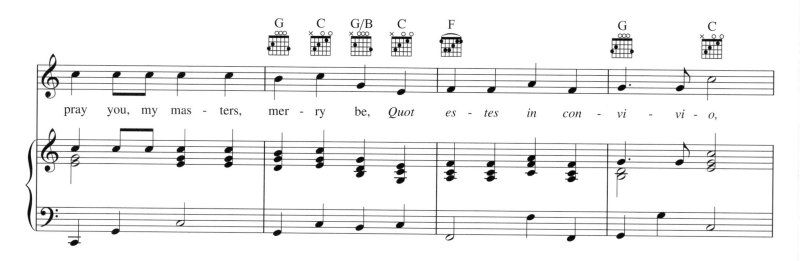

pray you, my mas - ters, mer - ry be, *Quot es - tes in con - vi - vi - o,*

BRING A TORCH, JEANNETTE ISABELLA

17th Century French Provençal Carol

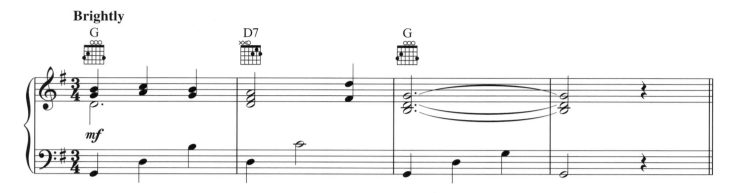

Bring a torch, _____ Jean - nette Is - a - bel - la,
Has - ten now, _____ good folk of the vil - lage,

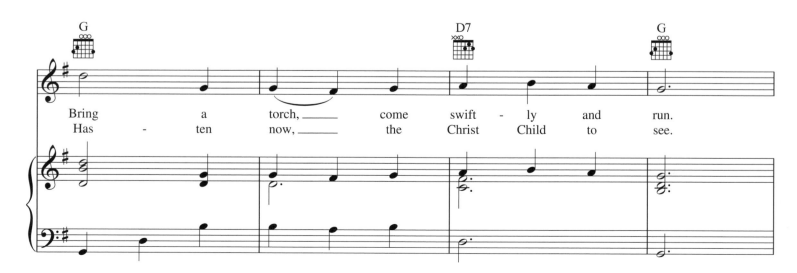

Bring a torch, _____ come swift - ly and run.
Has - ten now, _____ the Christ Child to see.

BURGUNDIAN CAROL

Words and Music by
OSCAR BRAND

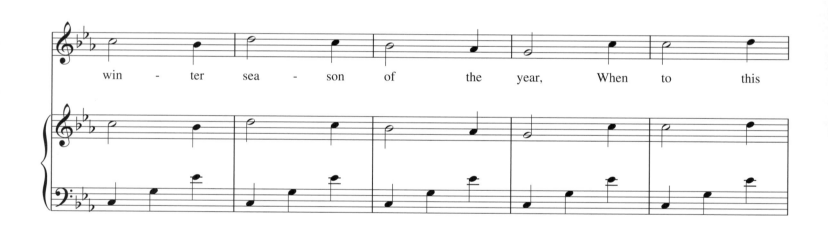

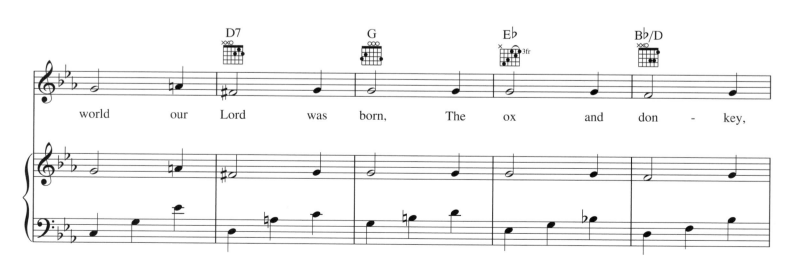

CAROL OF THE BELLS

Ukrainian Christmas Carol

Exuberantly

CHRISTMAS IS

Lyrics by SPENCE MAXWELL
Music by PERCY FAITH

THE CHIPMUNK SONG

Words and Music by
ROSS BAGDASARIAN

C-H-R-I-S-T-M-A-S

Words by JENNY LOU CARSON
Music by EDDY ARNOLD

When I was but a young-ster, Christ-mas meant one thing: that I'd be get-ting lots of toys that day.

I learned a whole lot dif-f'rent when Moth-er sat me

CHRISTMAS IS A-COMIN'
(May God Bless You)

Words and Music by
FRANK LUTHER

Moderately slow

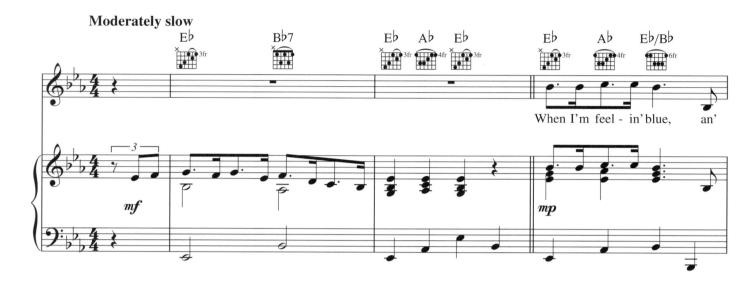

When I'm feel-in' blue, an'

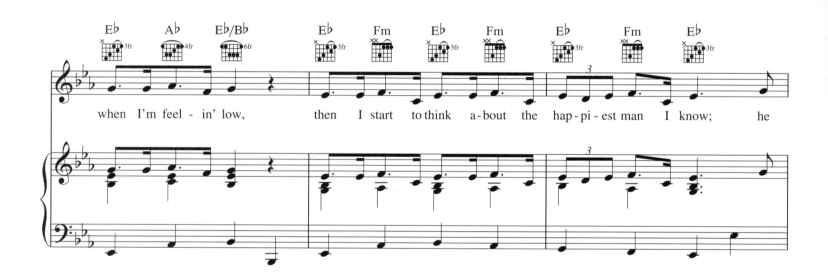

when I'm feel-in' low, then I start to think a-bout the hap-pi-est man I know; he

does-n't mind the snow an' he does-n't mind the rain, but all De-cem-ber you will hear him

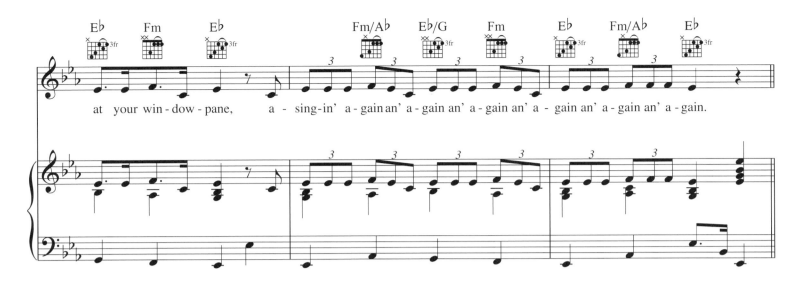

at your win-dow-pane, a - sing-in' a - gain an' a - gain an' a - gain an' a - gain an' a - gain an' a - gain.

Christ-mas is a-com-in' and the geese are get - tin' fat, please to put a pen-ny in a
Christ-mas is a-com-in' and the lights are on the tree, how a-bout a tur-key leg for
Christ-mas is a-com-in' and the egg is in the nog, please to let me sit a-round your

poor man's hat. If you have-n't got a pen-ny then a ha' pen-ny 'll do, if you
poor old me? If you have-n't got a tur-key leg, a tur-key wing 'll do, if you
old yule log. If you'd rath-er I did-n't sit a-round, to stand a-round 'll do, if you'd

52

have - n't got a ha' pen - ny, may God bless you. God bless you, gen - tle - men,
have - n't got a tur - key wing, may God bless you. God bless you, gen - tle - men,
rath - er I did - n't stand a - round, may God bless you. God bless you, gen - tle - men,

God bless you, if you have - n't got a ha' pen - ny, may God bless you.
God bless you, if you have - n't got a tur - key wing, may God bless you.
God bless you, if you'd rath - er I did - n't stand a - round, may

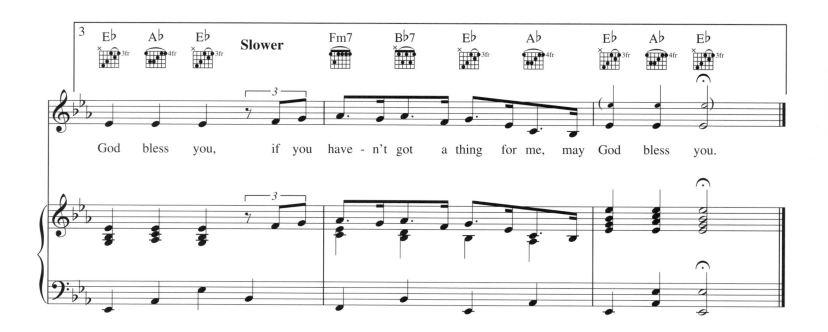

God bless you, if you have - n't got a thing for me, may God bless you.

THE CHRISTMAS SONG
(Chestnuts Roasting on an Open Fire)

Music and Lyric by MEL TORME
and ROBERT WELLS

55

CHRISTMAS TIME IS HERE

from A CHARLIE BROWN CHRISTMAS

Words by LEE MENDELSON
Music by VINCE GUARALDI

58

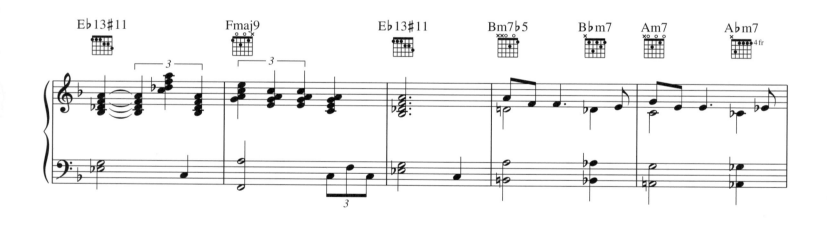

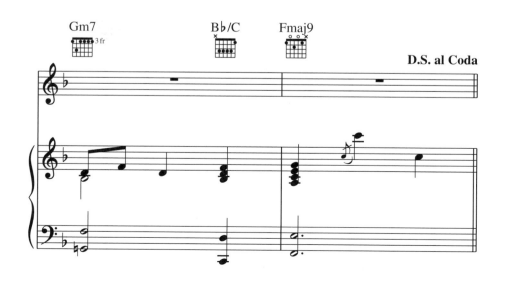

THE CHRISTMAS WALTZ

Words by SAMMY CAHN
Music by JULE STYNE

COME, ALL YE SHEPHERDS

Traditional Czech Text
Traditional Moravian Melody

COVENTRY CAROL

Words by ROBERT CROO
Traditional English Melody

Tenderly

1. Lul - lay, thou lit - tle ti - ny child, by by, lul -
2. O sis - ters too, how may we do, for to pre -
3., 4. *(See additional verses)*

ly lul - lay. _____ Lul - lay, thou lit - tle
serve this day. _____ This poor young - ling for

ti - ny child. By by, lul - ly, lul - lay. _____
whom we sing. By by, lul - ly, lul - lay. _____

Additional Verses

3. Herod the king,
   In his raging,
   Charged he hath this day.
   His men of might,
   In his own sight,
   All young children to slay.

4. That woe is me,
   Poor child for thee!
   And ever morn and day,
   For thy parting
   Neither say nor sing
   By by, lully lullay!

DECK THE HALL

Traditional Welsh Carol

65

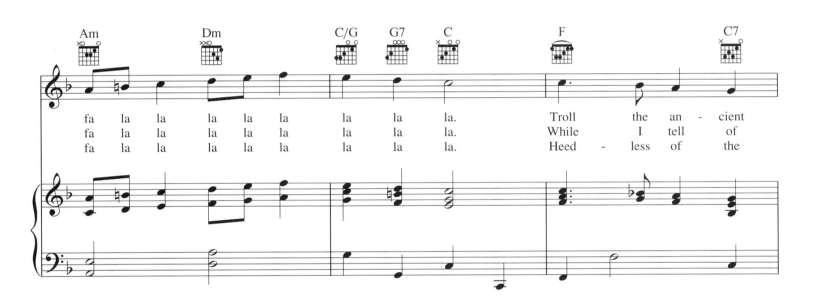

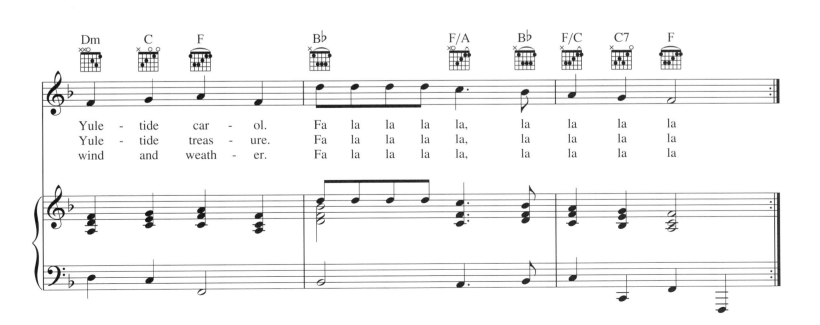

DING DONG! MERRILY ON HIGH!

French Carol

Ding dong! Mer - ri - ly on high in heav'n the bells are ring - ing.
E'en so here be - low, be - low, let stee - ple bells be swung - en,
Pray you, du - ti - ful - ly prime your mat - in chime, ye ring - ers.

Ding dong! Ver - i - ly the sky is riv'n with an - gel
And i - o, i - o, i - o, by priest and peo - ple
May you beau - ti - ful - ly rime your eve - time song, ye

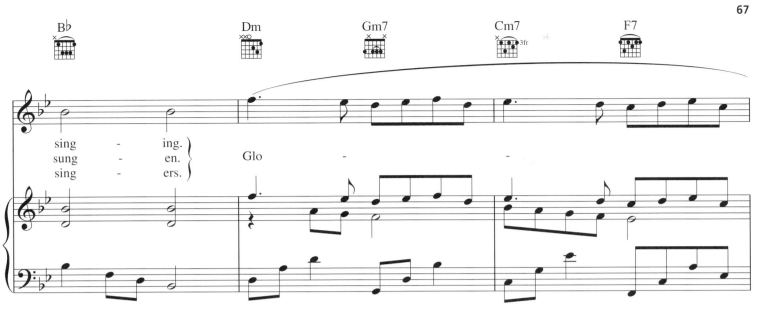

sing - ing.
sung - en.
sing - ers. Glo - - - - -

- - -

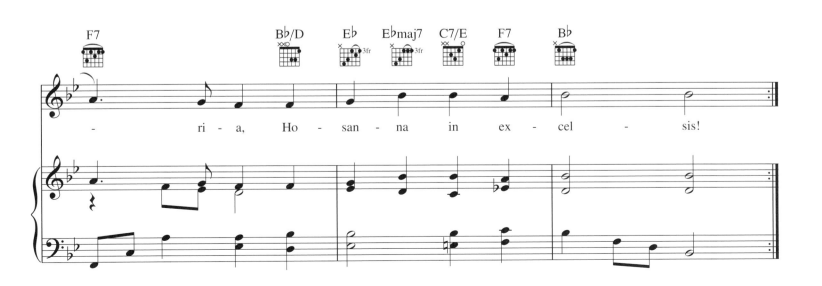

- ri - a, Ho - san - na in ex - cel - sis!

DO THEY KNOW IT'S CHRISTMAS?

Words and Music by M. URE
and B. GELDOF

DO YOU HEAR WHAT I HEAR

Words and Music by NOEL REGNEY
and GLORIA SHAYNE

EMMANUEL

Words and Music by
MICHAEL W. SMITH

Everyone's a Child at Christmas

Music and Lyrics by
JOHNNY MARKS

Ev - 'ry - one's a child at Christ - mas _____ and looks for pres - ents un - der the Christ - mas tree. _____ Ev - 'ry - one's a

FELIZ NAVIDAD

Music and Lyrics by
JOSÉ FELICIANO

FROSTY THE SNOW MAN

Words and Music by STEVE NELSON
and JACK ROLLINS

THE FIRST NOËL

17th Century English Carol
Music from W. Sandys' *Christmas Carols*

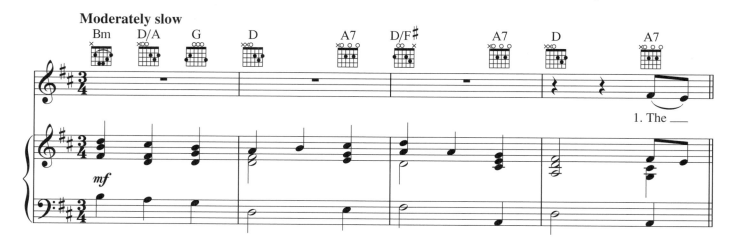

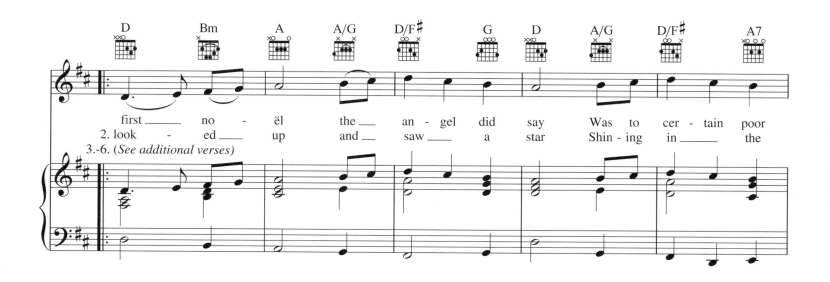

first no - ël the an - gel did say Was to cer - tain poor
2. look - ed up and saw a star Shin - ing in the
3.-6. *(See additional verses)*

shep - herds in fields as they lay; In fields where they lay
East, be - yond them far. And to the earth it

Additional Verses

3. And by the light of that same star,
   Three wise men came from country far.
   To seek for a King was their intent,
   And to follow the star wherever it went.
   Refrain

4. This star drew nigh to the northwest;
   O'er Bethlehem it took its rest.
   And there it did both stop and stay,
   Right over the place where Jesus lay.
   Refrain

5. Then entered in those wise men three,
   Full rev'rently upon their knee;
   And offered there in His presence,
   Their gold and myrrh and frankincense.
   Refrain

6. Then let us all with one accord
   Sing praises to our heav'nly Lord,
   That hath made heav'n and earth of naught,
   And with His blood mankind hath bought.
   Refrain

THE FRIENDLY BEASTS

Traditional English Carol

beasts   a - round   Him   stood,

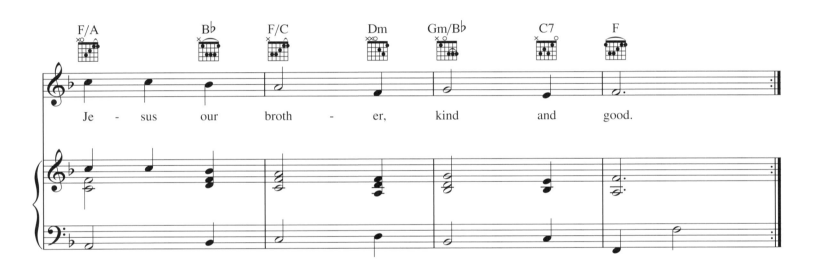

Je - sus our broth - er, kind and good.

Additional Verses

2. "I," said the donkey, shaggy and brown,
   "I carried His mother up hill and down;
   I carried her safely to Bethlehem town."
   "I," said the donkey, shaggy and brown.

3. "I," said the cow all white and red,
   "I gave Him my manger for His bed;
   I gave him my hay to pillow His head."
   "I," said the cow all white and red.

4. "I," said the sheep with curly horn,
   "I gave Him my wool for His blanket warm;
   He wore my coat on Christmas morn."
   "I," said the sheep with curly horn.

5. "I," said the dove from the rafters high,
   "I cooed Him to sleep so He would not cry;
   We cooed Him to sleep, my mate and I."
   "I," said the dove from the rafters high.

6. Thus every beast by some good spell,
   In the stable dark was glad to tell
   Of the gift he gave Emmanuel,
   The gift he gave Emmanuel.

FUM, FUM, FUM

Traditional Catalonian Carol

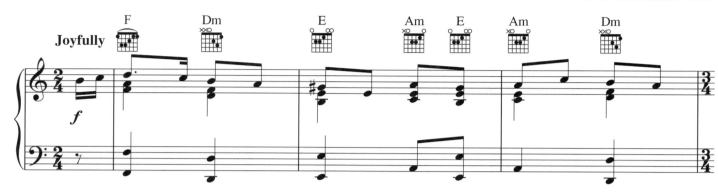

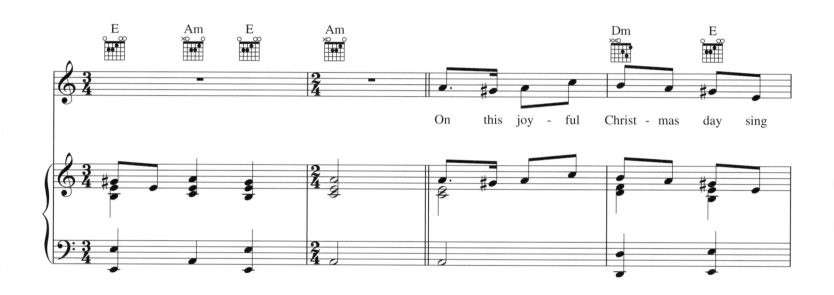

On this joy - ful Christ - mas day sing

Fum, Fum, Fum. On this joy - ful Christ - mas day sing

GOIN' ON A SLEIGHRIDE

Words and Music by
RALPH BLANE

100

GLAD TIDINGS
(Shalom Chaverim)

English Lyrics and New Music Arranged by RONNIE GILBERT,
LEE HAYS, FRED HELLERMAN and PETE SEEGER

GO, TELL IT ON THE MOUNTAIN

African-American Spiritual
Verses by JOHN W. WORK, JR.

GOD REST YE MERRY, GENTLEMEN

19th Century English Carol

God rest ye mer - ry, gen - tle - men, let
Beth - le - hem, in Jew - ry let this
God our Heav'n - ly Fa - ther A

noth - ing you dis - may, For Je - sus Christ our
bless - ed Babe was born, And laid with - in a
bless - ed an - gel came, And un - to cer - tain

Sav - ior was born up - on this day, To
man - ger, Up - on this bless - ed morn; To
shep - herds brought tid - ings of the same; How

GOOD CHRISTIAN MEN, REJOICE

14th Century Latin Text
Translated by JOHN MASON NEALE
14th Century German Melody

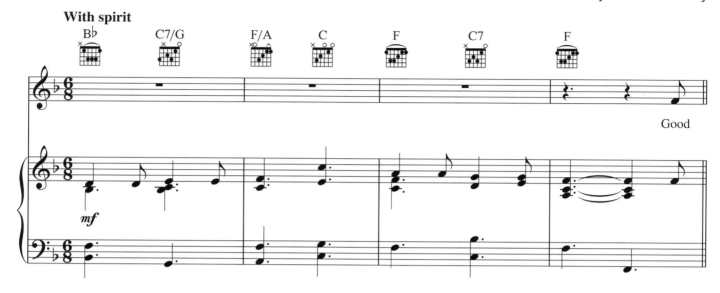

With spirit

Good

Chris - tian men, re - joice _____ with heart and soul and
Chris - tian men, re - joice _____ with heart and soul and

voice, _____ Give ye heed to what we say:
voice, _____ Now ye hear of end - less bliss;

THE GREATEST GIFT OF ALL

Words and Music by
JOHN JARVIS

112

GREENWILLOW CHRISTMAS

from GREENWILLOW

By FRANK LOESSER

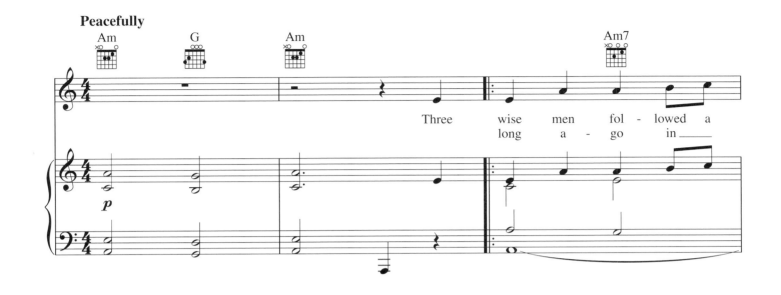

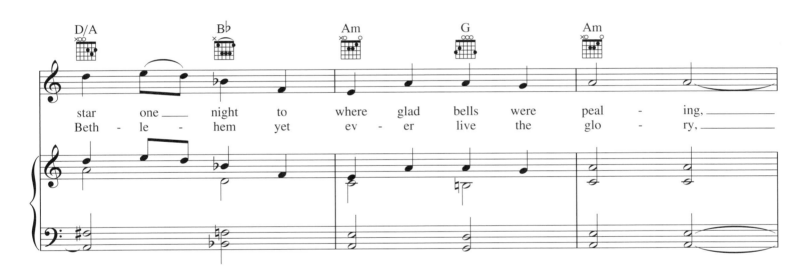

HAPPY HANUKKAH, MY FRIEND
(The Hanukkah Song)

Words and Music by JUSTIN WILDE
and DOUGLAS ALAN KONECKY

Spin the drei-del, light the lights,
Can-dle-light or star a-bove,

ev-'ry-one stay home to-night.
mes-sag-es of peace and love;

The sto-ry is told, __ the
their mean-ing is clear, __ we

HAPPY HOLIDAY

from the Motion Picture Irving Berlin's HOLIDAY INN

Words and Music by
IRVING BERLIN

HE

Words by RICHARD MULLEN
Music by JACK RICHARDS

HAPPY XMAS
(War Is Over)

Words and Music by JOHN LENNON
and YOKO ONO

So this is X-mas, and what have you done?
X-mas, and what have we done?

An-oth-er year o-ver, a new one just be-
An-oth-er year o-ver, a new one just be-

gun. ____ And so this is X-mas; I hope you have
gun. ____ And so hap-py X-mas; we hope you have

HARD CANDY CHRISTMAS

Words and Music by
CAROL HALL

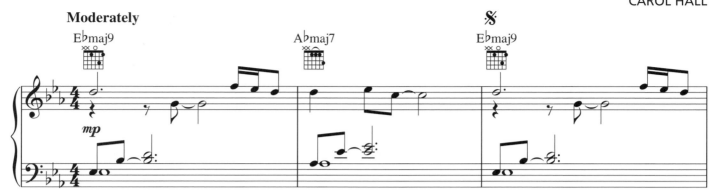

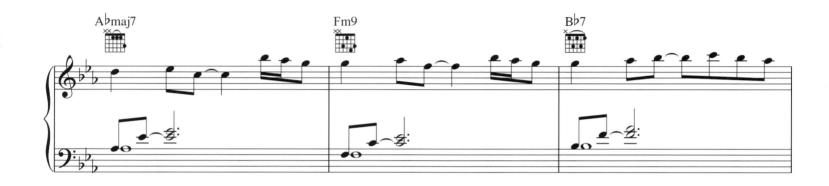

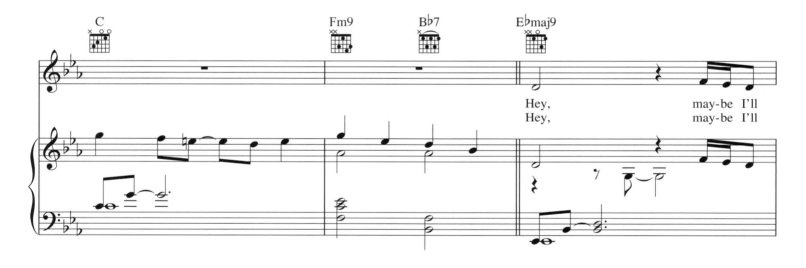

Hey,   may-be I'll
Hey,   may-be I'll

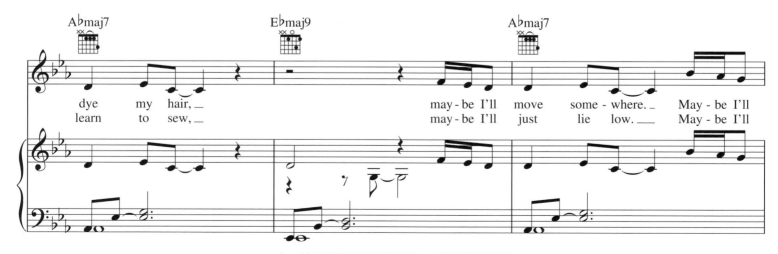

dye   my   hair,   may-be I'll move some-where.__ May-be I'll
learn to   sew,__   may-be I'll just lie low.___ May-be I'll

HARK! THE HERALD ANGELS SING

Words by CHARLES WESLEY
Altered by GEORGE WHITEFIELD
Music by FELIX MENDELSSOHN-BARTHOLDY
Arranged by WILLIAM H. CUMMINGS

Hark! The her - ald an - gels sing,____
Christ, by high - est heav'n a - dored,____
Hail, the heav'n - born Prince of Peace!____

"Glo - ry to the new - born King!
Christ, the ev - er - last - ing Lord;
Hail, the Sun of Right - eous - ness!

Peace on earth, and
Late in time be -
Light and life to

mer - cy mild,____ God and sin - ners rec - on - ciled."
hold Him come,____ Off - spring of the vir - gin's womb.
all He brings,____ Ris'n with heal - ing in His wings.

HERE WE COME A-WASSAILING

Traditional

Brightly

1. Here we come a-was-sail-ing A-mong the leaves so
2. We are not dai-ly beg-gars that beg from door to
3., 4. *(See additional verses)*

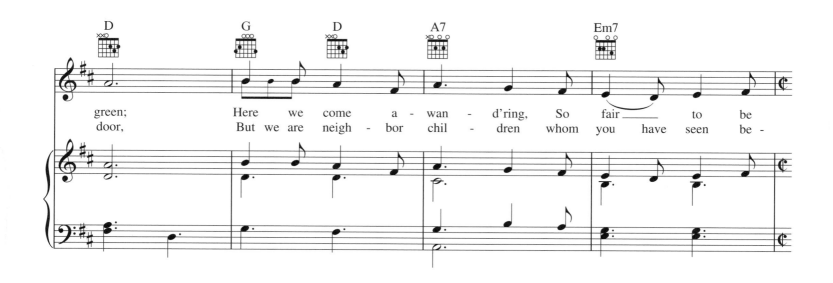

green; Here we come a-wan-d'ring, So fair___ to be
door, But we are neigh-bor chil-dren whom you have seen be-

(♩. = ♪) **Refrain**

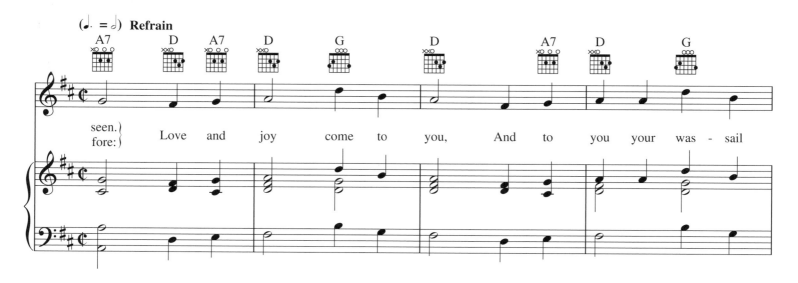

seen. } Love and joy come to you, And to you your was-sail
fore: }

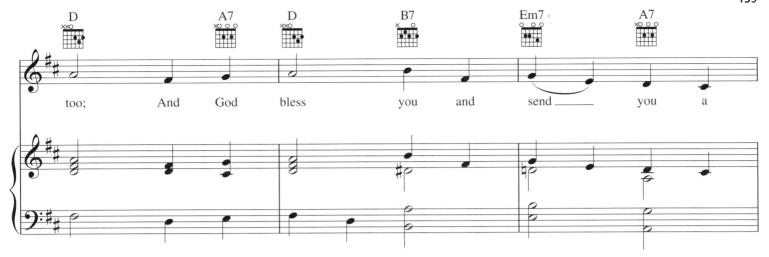

too; And God bless you and send ___ you a

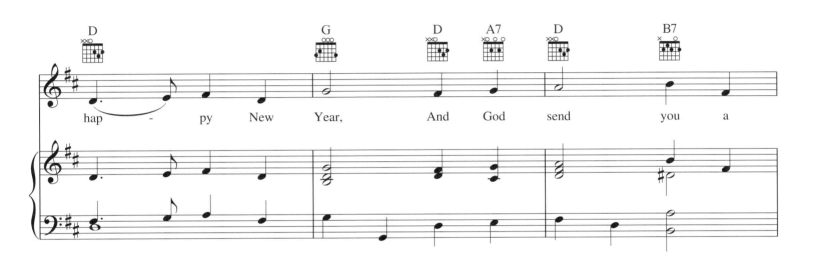

hap - py New Year, And God send you a

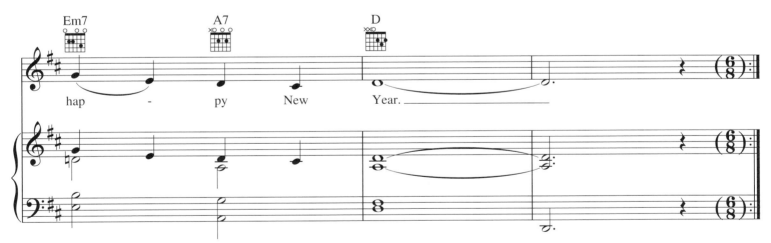

hap - py New Year. ___

Additional Verses

3. We have got a little purse
   Of stretching leather skin;
   We want a little money
   To line it well within:
   Refrain

4. God bless the master of this house,
   Likewise the mistress too;
   And all the little children
   That round the table go:
   Refrain

A HOLLY JOLLY CHRISTMAS

Music and Lyrics by
JOHNNY MARKS

141

(There's No Place Like)
HOME FOR THE HOLIDAYS

Words by AL STILLMAN
Music by ROBERT ALLEN

Moderately, with feeling

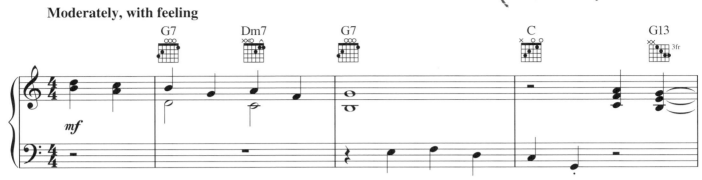

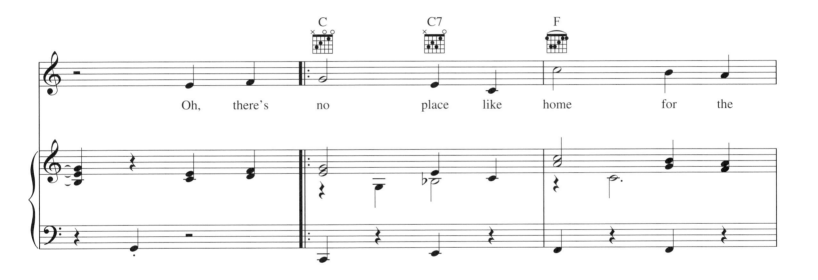

Oh, there's no place like home for the

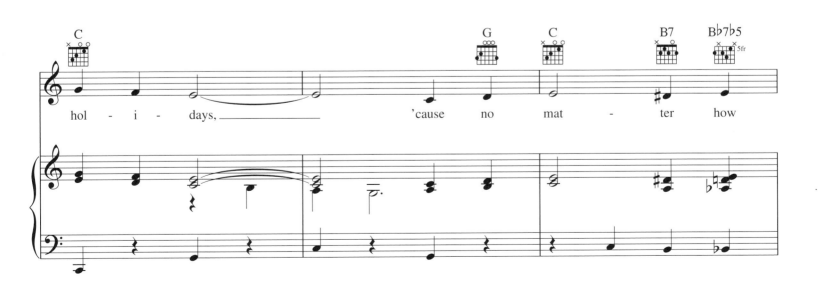

hol - i - days, _____ 'cause no mat - ter how

145

I HEARD THE BELLS ON CHRISTMAS DAY

Words by HENRY WADSWORTH LONGFELLOW
Music by JOHN BAPTISTE CALKIN

Additional Verses

3. And in despair I bowed my head:
   "There is no peace on earth," I said,
   "For hate is strong, and mocks the song
   Of peace on earth, good will to men."

4. Then pealed the bells more loud and deep:
   "God is not dead, nor doth He sleep;
   The wrong shall fail, the right prevail,
   With peace on earth, good will to men."

5. Till, ringing, singing on its way,
   The world revolved from night to day,
   A voice, a chime, a chant sublime,
   Of peace on earth, good will to men!

I SAW MOMMY KISSING SANTA CLAUS

Words and Music by
TOMMIE CONNOR

150

I HEARD THE BELLS ON CHRISTMAS DAY

Words by HENRY WADSWORTH LONGFELLOW
Adapted by JOHNNY MARKS
Music by JOHNNY MARKS

I SAW THREE SHIPS

Traditional English Carol

I'LL BE HOME FOR CHRISTMAS

Words and Music by KIM GANNON
and WALTER KENT

I WISH EVERYDAY COULD BE LIKE CHRISTMAS

Words and Music by DAVID ERWIN
and JIM CARTER

161

I'VE GOT MY LOVE TO KEEP ME WARM

from the 20th Century Fox Motion Picture ON THE AVENUE

Words and Music by
IRVING BERLIN

Bright jump tempo

The snow is snow-ing, the wind is blow-ing, but I can weath-er the storm.

What do I care how much it may storm?

INFANT HOLY, INFANT LOWLY

Traditional Polish Carol
Paraphrased by EDITH M.G. REED

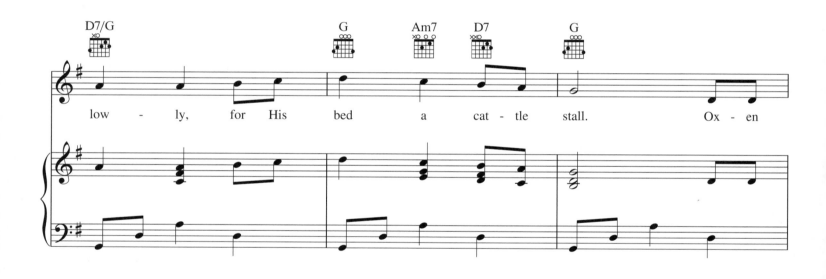

IT CAME UPON THE MIDNIGHT CLEAR

Words by EDMUND HAMILTON SEARS
Music by RICHARD STORRS WILLIS

IT MUST HAVE BEEN THE MISTLETOE
(Our First Christmas)

By JUSTIN WILDE
and DOUG KONECKY

IT'S BEGINNING TO LOOK LIKE CHRISTMAS

By MEREDITH WILLSON

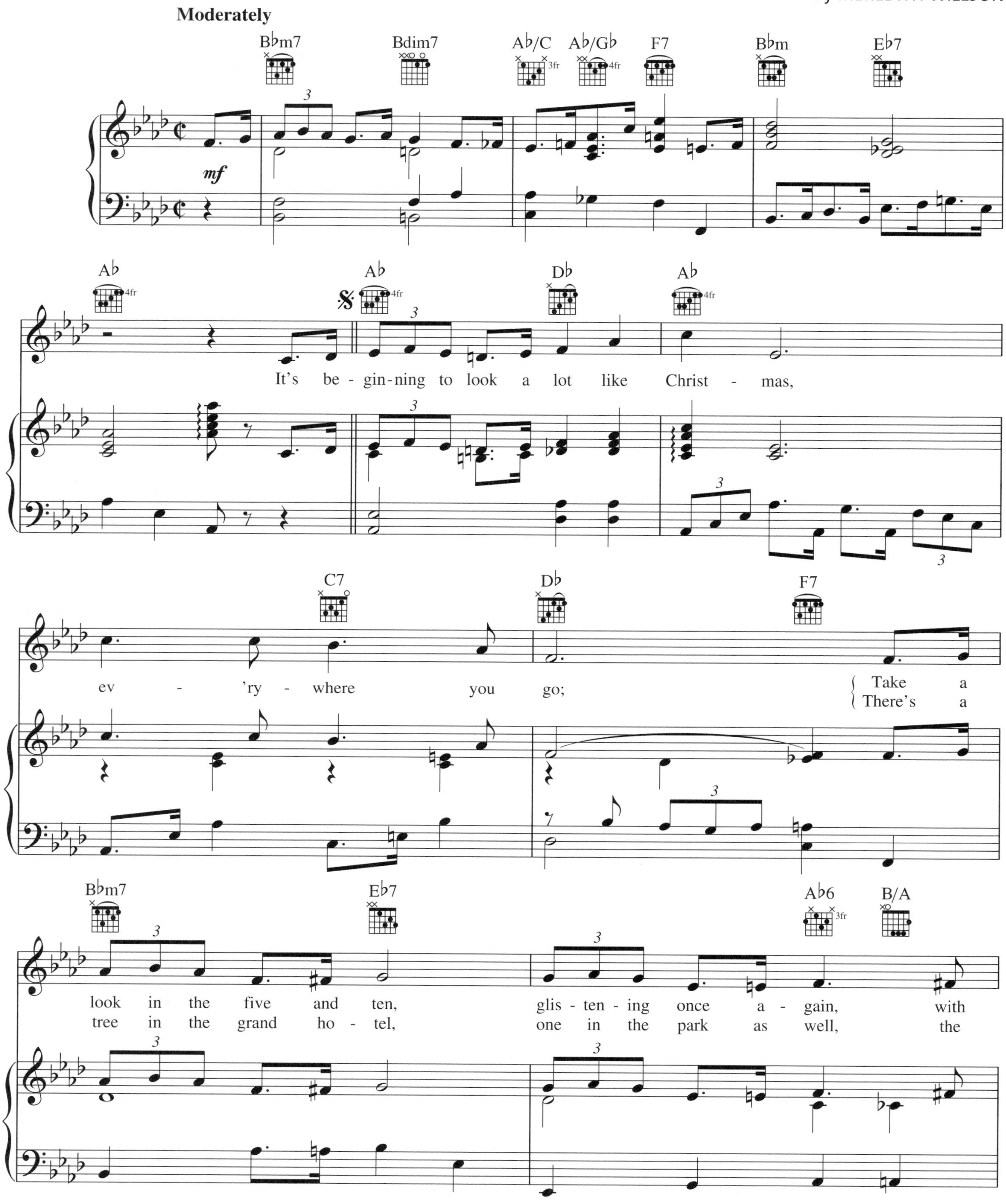

Moderately
B♭m7
Bdim7
A♭/C
A♭/G♭
F7
B♭m
E♭7
mf
A♭
A♭
D♭
A♭
It's be - gin - ning to look a lot like Christ - mas,
C7
D♭
F7
ev - 'ry - where you go;
Take a
There's a
B♭m7
E♭7
A♭6
B/A
look in the five and ten, glis - ten - ing once a - gain, with
tree in the grand ho - tel, one in the park as well, the

IT'S CHRISTMAS IN NEW YORK

Words and Music by
BILLY BUTT

fill - ing each yearn - ing, ___ it's Christ-mas in New _

York.

IT'S JUST ANOTHER
NEW YEARS'S EVE

Lyric by MARTY PANZER
Music by BARRY MANILOW

Slow Ballad

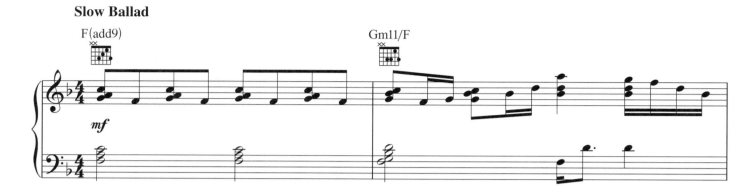

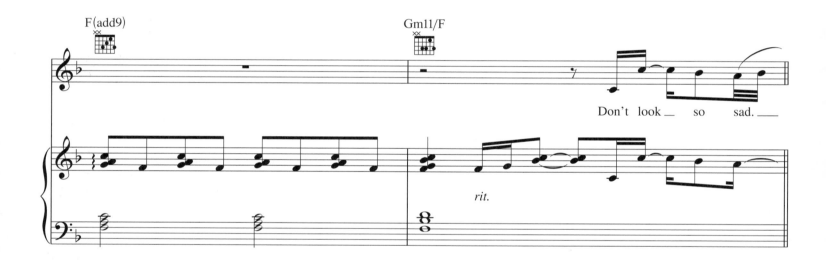

Don't look __ so sad. __

__
__ lone,

It's not __ so bad, __ you know. __
but we've __ made good __ friends, too. __
we've got __ the world, __ you know. __

It's just an-oth-er
Re-mem-ber all the
And it won't let us

night,
nights _____
down,

that's all it is. _____
we've _ spent with them
just wait and see. _____

It's not ___ the first. ___
and all our plans. _
And we'll _ grow old,

___
___ Who says ___ they can't _ come true? ___
___ but think _ how wise _ we'll grow. ___

It's not the worst, _ you know. _
We've come through all _____
To - night's an - oth -
There's more, you know, _

___ the rest.
We'll get through this. ___
We've made _ mis - takes _

188

JINGLE-BELL ROCK

Words and Music by JOE BEAL
and JIM BOOTHE

JINGLE BELLS

Words and Music by
J. PIERPONT

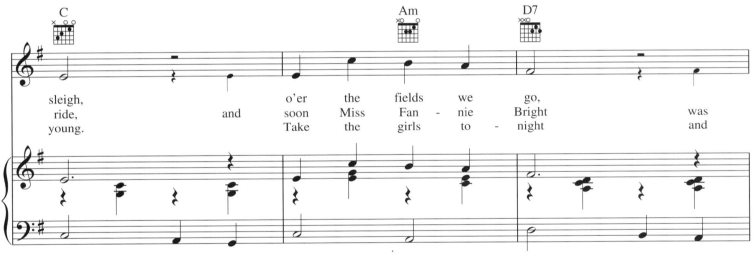

194

JINGLE, JINGLE, JINGLE

Music and Lyrics by
JOHNNY MARKS

JOLLY OLD ST. NICHOLAS

Traditional 19th Century American Carol

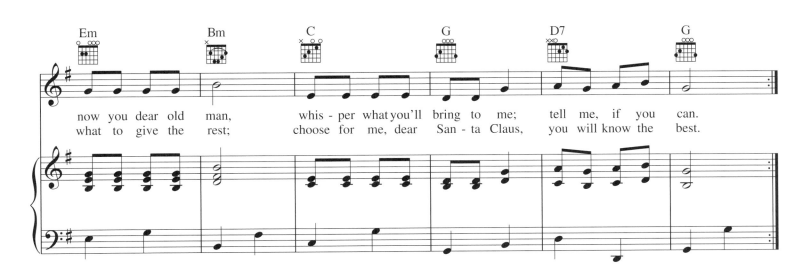

JOY TO THE WORLD

Words by ISAAC WATTS
Music by GEORGE FRIDERIC HANDEL
Arranged by LOWELL MASON

With spirit

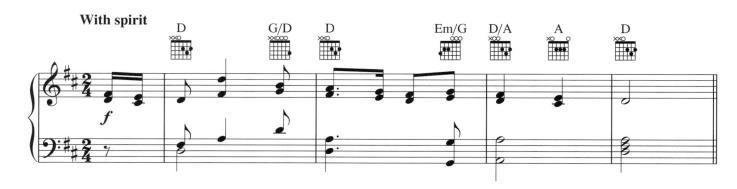

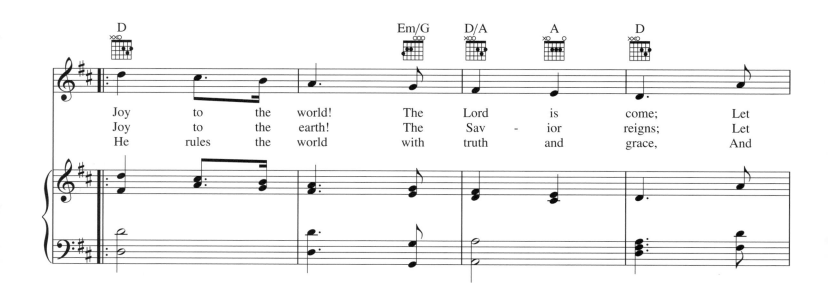

Joy to the world! The Lord is come; Let
Joy to the world! The Sav - ior reigns; Let
He rules the world with truth and grace, Let

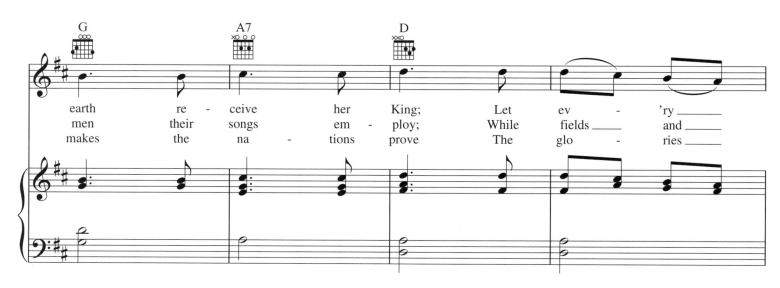

earth re - ceive her King; Let ev - 'ry
men their songs em - ploy; While fields and
makes the na - tions prove The glo - ries

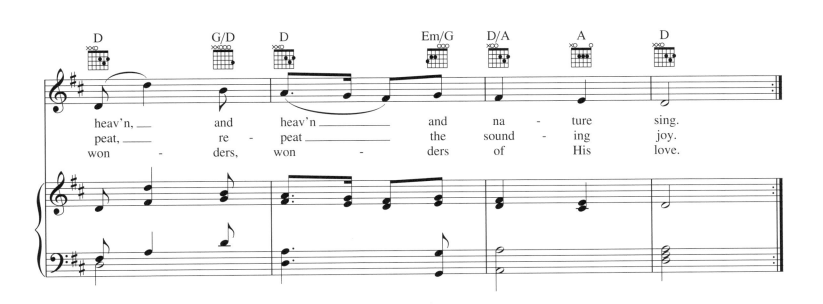

JOYOUS CHRISTMAS

Music and Lyrics by
JOHNNY MARKS

203

THE LAST MONTH OF THE YEAR
(What Month Was Jesus Born In?)

Words and Music by VERA HALL
Adapted and Arranged by RUBY PICKENS TARTT
and ALAN LOMAX

LAST CHRISTMAS

Words and Music by
GEORGE MICHAEL

211

LET IT SNOW! LET IT SNOW! LET IT SNOW!

Words by SAMMY CAHN
Music by JULE STYNE

LET'S HAVE AN
OLD FASHIONED CHRISTMAS

Lyric by LARRY CONLEY
Music by JOE SOLOMON

A MARSHMALLOW WORLD

Words by CARL SIGMAN
Music by PETER DE ROSE

LITTLE SAINT NICK

Words and Music by BRIAN WILSON
and MIKE LOVE

Moderately fast

Ooh, Mer - ry Christ - mas, Saint

Nick. (Christ - mas comes this time each year.) Ooh.

Well, way up north where the
lit - tle bob - sled, we call it
haul - in' through the snow at a

*Recorded one half-step lower.

223

LO, HOW A ROSE E'ER BLOOMING

15th Century German Carol
Translated by THEODORE BAKER
Music from *Alte Catholische Geistliche Kirchengesäng*

Tenderly

Lo, how a rose e'er bloom - ing From ten - der stem _____ hath sprung! Of Jes - se's lin - eage com - ing As men of old _____ have sung. It came, a flow'r - et bright, A - mid the cold of win -

MASTERS IN THIS HALL

Traditional English

Energetically

Mas - ters in this hall, _____ Hear ye news to - day, _____ Brought from o - ver sea, And ev - er I you pray.

MERRY CHRISTMAS, DARLING

Words and Music by RICHARD CARPENTER
and FRANK POOLER

Greet-ing cards have all been sent, the Christ-mas rush is through,

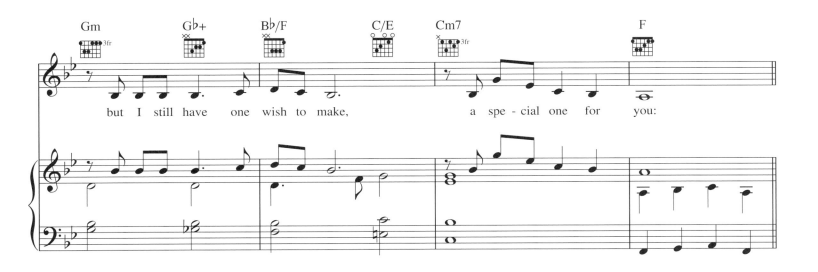

but I still have one wish to make, a spe-cial one for you:

Mer-ry Christ-mas, dar-ling. We're a-part, that's true; but

THE MERRY CHRISTMAS POLKA

Words by PAUL FRANCIS WEBSTER
Music by SONNY BURKE

Moderate Polka tempo

They're

tun - ing up the fid - dles now, the fid - dles now, the fid - dles now. There's

wine to warm the mid - dles now and set your head a - whirl. A-

236

A MERRY, MERRY CHRISTMAS TO YOU

Music and Lyrics by
JOHNNY MARKS

Very spirited

Mer - ry, Mer - ry, Mer - ry, Mer - ry, Mer - ry Christ - mas to you. ____ May each day be ver - y, ver - y hap - py all the year through. ____

*Use any language desired.

(*) *Can repeat full chorus then 4 bar vamp shouting languages, then Coda.*

MISTER SANTA

Words and Music by
PAT BALLARD

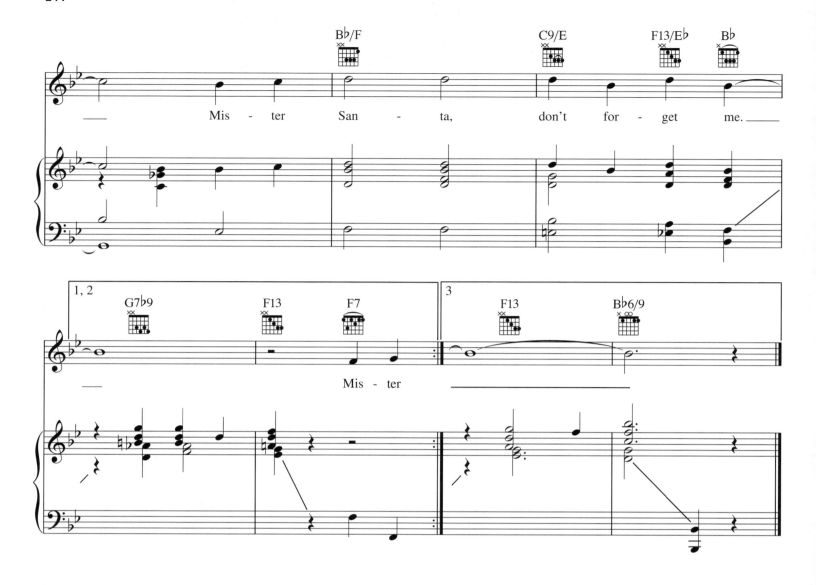

Additional Lyrics

2. Mister Santa, dear old Saint Nick,
   Be awful careful and please don't get sick.
   Put on your coat when breezes are blowin',
   And when you cross the street look where you're goin'.
   Santa, we (I) love you so,
   We (I) hope you never get lost in the snow.
   Take your time when you unpack,
   Mister Santa, don't hurry back.

3. Mister Santa, we've been so good;
   We've washed the dishes and done what we should.
   Made up the beds and scrubbed up our toesies,
   We've used a kleenex when we've blown our nosesies.
   Santa, look at our ears, they're clean as whistles,
   We're sharper than shears.
   Now we've put you on the spot,
   Mister Santa, bring us a lot.

THE NIGHT BEFORE CHRISTMAS SONG

Music by JOHNNY MARKS
Lyrics adapted by JOHNNY MARKS
from CLEMENT MOORE'S Poem

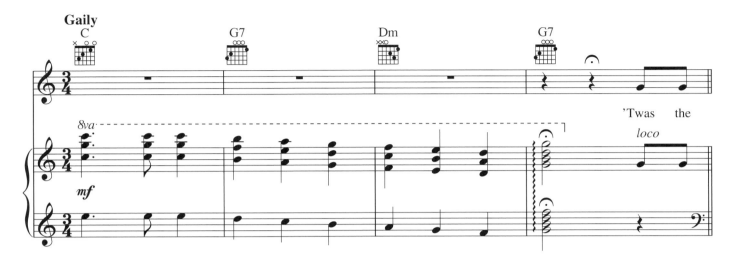

night be-fore Christ-mas and all thru the house, not a crea-ture was
up to the house-top the rein-deer soon flew, with the sleigh full of

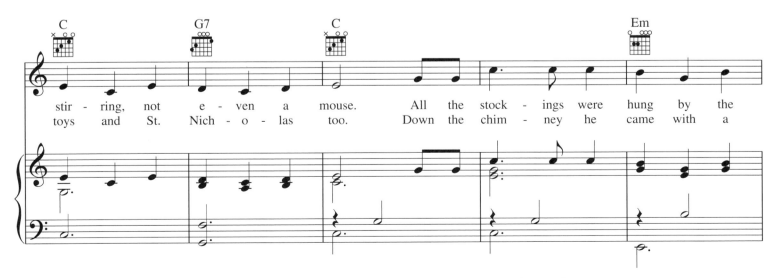

stir-ring, not e-ven a mouse. All the stock-ings were hung by the
toys and St. Nich-o-las too. Down the chim-ney he came with a

THE MOST WONDERFUL DAY OF THE YEAR

Music and Lyrics by
JOHNNY MARKS

MY FAVORITE THINGS

from THE SOUND OF MUSIC

Lyrics by OSCAR HAMMERSTEIN II
Music by RICHARD RODGERS

NUTTIN' FOR CHRISTMAS

Words and Music by ROY BENNETT
and SID TEPPER

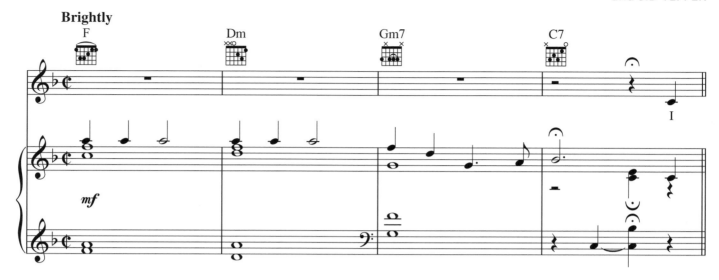

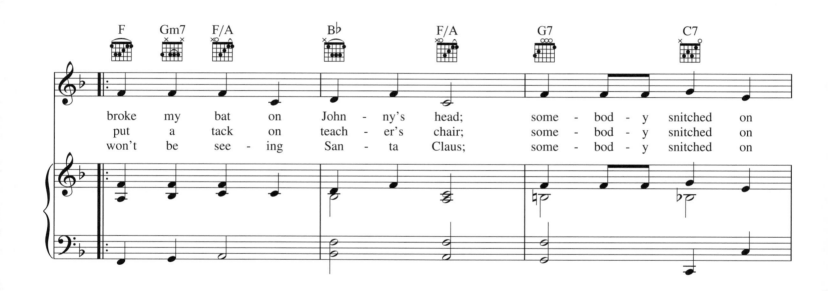

broke my bat on John-ny's head; some-bod-y snitched on
put a tack on teach-er's chair; some-bod-y snitched on
won't be see-ing San-ta Claus; some-bod-y snitched on

me. I hid a frog in sis-ter's bed;
me. I tied a knot in Su-sie's hair;
me. He won't come vis-it me be-cause

O CHRISTMAS TREE

Traditional German Carol

O COME, ALL YE FAITHFUL
(Adeste Fideles)

Words and Music by JOHN FRANCIS WADE
Latin Words translated by FREDERICK OAKELEY

263

O COME, LITTLE CHILDREN

Words by C. VON SCHMIDT
Music by J.P.A. SCHULZ

come, lit - tle chil - dren, from cot and from hall, O

come to the man - ger in Beth - le - hem's stall. There

meek - ly He li - eth, the heav - en - ly Child, So

O COME, O COME IMMANUEL

Plainsong, 13th Century
Words translated by JOHN M. NEALE
and HENRY S. COFFIN

Moderately slow, in 2

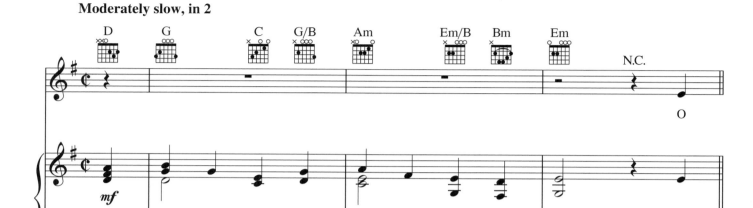

268

AN OLD FASHIONED CHRISTMAS

Music and Lyrics by
JOHNNY MARKS

O HOLY NIGHT

French Words by PLACIDE CAPPEAU
English Words by JOHN S. DWIGHT
Music by ADOLPHE ADAM

273

O LITTLE TOWN OF BETHLEHEM

Words by PHILLIPS BROOKS
Music by LEWIS H. REDNER

OLD TOY TRAINS

Words and Music by
ROGER MILLER

ONE BRIGHT STAR

Words and Music by
JOHN JARVIS

ONCE IN ROYAL DAVID'S CITY

Words by CECIL F. ALEXANDER
Music by HENRY J. GAUNTLETT

PARADE OF THE WOODEN SOLDIERS

English Lyrics by BALLARD MacDONALD
Music by LEON JESSEL

PRETTY PAPER

Words and Music by
WILLIE NELSON

ROCKIN' AROUND THE CHRISTMAS TREE

Music and Lyrics by
JOHNNY MARKS

RUDOLPH THE RED-NOSED REINDEER

Music and Lyrics by
JOHNNY MARKS

SANTA BABY

By JOAN JAVITS,
PHIL SPRINGER and TONY SPRINGER

SANTA CLAUS IS COMIN' TO TOWN

Words by HAVEN GILLESPIE
Music by J. FRED COOTS

SANTA, BRING MY BABY BACK
(To Me)

Words and Music by CLAUDE DeMETRUIS
and AARON SCHROEDER

SHAKE ME I RATTLE
(Squeeze Me I Cry)

Words and Music by HAL HACKADY
and CHARLES NAYLOR

314

SING WE NOW OF CHRISTMAS

Traditional

Sing we now of Christ - mas, No - ël sing we here. Sing our grate - ful prais - es To the maid so dear.

SILENT NIGHT

Words by JOSEPH MOHR
Translated by JOHN F. YOUNG
Music by FRANZ X. GRUBER

SILVER AND GOLD

Music and Lyrics by
JOHNNY MARKS

SILVER BELLS
from the Paramount Picture THE LEMON DROP KID

Words and Music by JAY LIVINGSTON
and RAY EVANS

323

SOME CHILDREN SEE HIM

Lyric by WIHLA HUTSON
Music by ALFRED BURT

SOME THINGS FOR CHRISTMAS
(A Snake, Some Mice, Some Glue and a Hole Too)

Lyric by JACQUELYN REINACH and JOAN LAMPORT
Music by JACQUELYN REINACH

STILL, STILL, STILL

Salzburg Melody, c.1819
Traditional Austrian Text

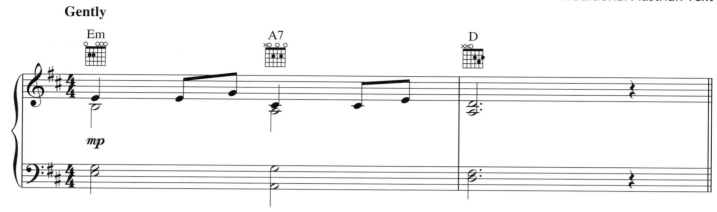

Still, ____ still, ____ still; to ____ sleep is ____ now His ____
Sleep, ____ sleep, ____ sleep, while ____ we Thy ____ vig - il ____

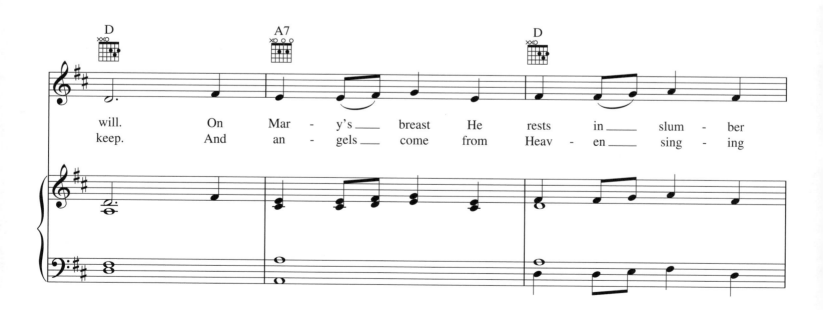

will. On Mar - y's ____ breast He rests in ____ slum - ber
keep. And an - gels ____ come He from Heav - en ____ sing - ing

SUZY SNOWFLAKE

Words and Music by SID TEPPER
and ROY BENNETT

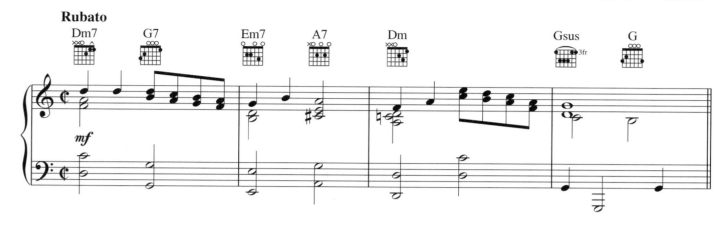

Here comes Su - zy Snow - flake, dressed in a snow - white
Here comes Su - zy Snow - flake, soon you will hear her

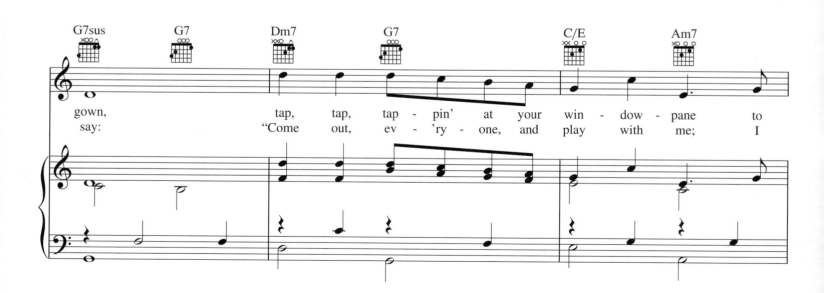

gown, tap, tap, tap - pin' at your win - dow - pane to
say: "Come out, ev - 'ry - one, and play with me; I

TENNESSEE CHRISTMAS

Words and Music by AMY GRANT
and GARY CHAPMAN

THAT CHRISTMAS FEELING

Words and Music by BENNIE BENJAMIN
and GEORGE WEISS

344

TOYLAND
from BABES IN TOYLAND

Words by GLEN MacDONOUGH
Music by VICTOR HERBERT

THIS ONE'S FOR THE CHILDREN

Words and Music by
MAURICE STARR

348

Repeat and Fade

'TWAS THE NIGHT BEFORE CHRISTMAS

Words by CLEMENT CLARK MOORE
Music by F. HENRI KLICKMAN

Additional Verses

3. With a little old driver so lively and quick,
   I knew in a moment it must be St. Nick.
   More rapid than eagles his coursers they came,
   And he whistled, and shouted, and called them by name:
   "Now, Dasher! Now, Dancer! Now, Prancer! Now Vixen!
   On, Comet! On, Cupid, On Donder and Blitzen!
   To the top of the porch, to the top of the wall!
   Now dash away, dash away, dash away all!"

4. As dry leaves that before the wild hurricane fly,
   When they meet with an obstacle, mount to the sky,
   So up to the house-top the coursers they flew,
   With the sleigh full of toys, and St. Nicholas, too.
   And then in a twinkling I heard on the roof
   The prancing and pawing of each little hoof.
   As I drew in my head, and was turning around,
   Down the chimney St. Nicholas came with a bound.

5. He was dressed all in fur from his head to his foot,
   And his clothes were all tarnished with ashes and soot;
   A bundle of toys he had flung on his back,
   And he looked like a peddler just opening his pack.
   His eyes how they twinkled! His dimples how merry!
   His cheeks were like roses, his nose like a cherry.
   His droll little mouth was drawn up like a bow,
   And the beard of his chin was as white as the snow.

6. The stump of a pipe he held tight in his teeth,
   And the smoke, it encircled his head like a wreath.
   He had a broad face, and a round little belly
   That shook, when he laughed, like a bowl full of jelly.
   He was chubby and plump, a right jolly old elf,
   And I laughed when I saw him, in spite of myself.
   A wink of his eye, and a twist of his head,
   Soon gave me to know I had nothing to dread.

7. He spoke not a word, but went straight to his work,
   And filled all the stockings; then turned with a jerk,
   And laying his finger aside of his nose,
   And giving a nod, up the chimney he rose.
   He sprang to his sleigh, to his team gave a whistle,
   And away they all fled like the down of a thistle;
   But I heard him exclaim, ere he drove out of sight:
   "Happy Christmas to all, and to all a Good-night!"

THE TWELVE DAYS OF CHRISTMAS

Traditional English Carol

On the first day of Christ-mas, my true love gave to me a par-tridge _ in a pear tree.

On the sec-ond day of Christ-mas, my true love sent to me:
third _ day of Christ-mas, my true love sent to me:
fourth _ day of Christ-mas, my true love sent to me:

UP ON THE HOUSETOP

Words and Music by
B.R. HANDY

WE ARE SANTA'S ELVES

Music and Lyrics by
JOHNNY MARKS

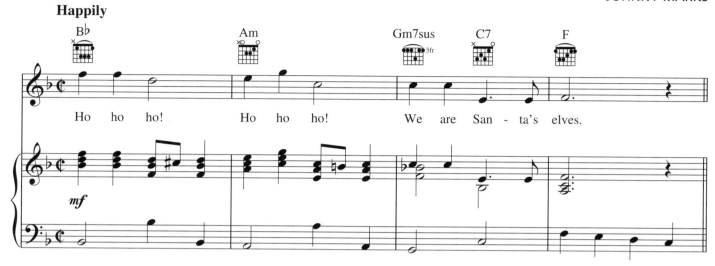

Ho ho ho! Ho ho ho! We are San - ta's elves.

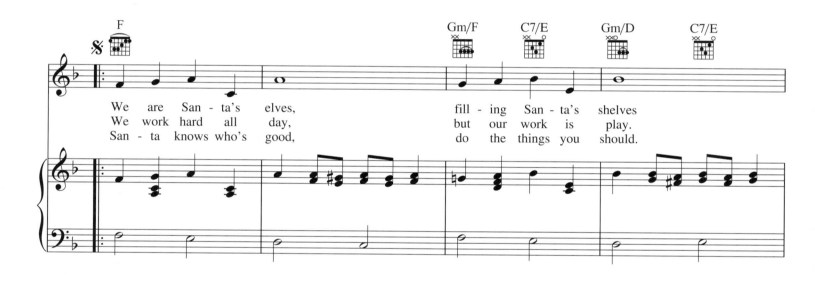

We are San - ta's elves, fill - ing San - ta's shelves
We work hard all day, but our work is play.
San - ta knows who's good, do the things you should.

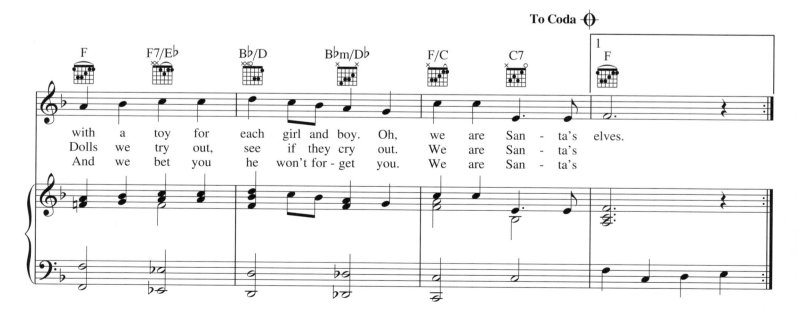

with a toy for each girl and boy. Oh, we are San - ta's elves.
Dolls we try out, see if they cry out. We are San - ta's
And we bet you he won't for - get you. We are San - ta's

WE NEED A LITTLE CHRISTMAS

from MAME

Music and Lyric by
JERRY HERMAN

WE WISH YOU A MERRY CHRISTMAS

Traditional English Folksong

WE THREE KINGS OF ORIENT ARE

Words and Music by
JOHN H. HOPKINS, JR.

WHAT ARE YOU DOING NEW YEAR'S EVE?

By FRANK LOESSER

WHAT CHILD IS THIS?

Words by WILLIAM C. DIX
16th Century English Melody

WHEN SANTA CLAUS GETS YOUR LETTER

Music and Lyrics by
JOHNNY MARKS

WONDERFUL CHRISTMASTIME

Words and Music by
McCARTNEY

YOU'RE ALL I WANT FOR CHRISTMAS

Words and Music by GLEN MOORE
and SEGER ELLIS